IN THE
NATIONAL INTEREST

General Sir John Monash once exhorted a graduating class to 'equip yourself for life, not solely for your own benefit but for the benefit of the whole community'. At the university established in his name, we repeat this statement to our own graduating classes, to acknowledge how important it is that common or public good flows from education.

Universities spread and build on the knowledge they acquire through scholarship in many ways, well beyond the transmission of this learning through education. It is a necessary part of a university's role to debate its findings, not only with other researchers and scholars, but also with the broader community in which it resides.

Publishing for the benefit of society is an important part of a university's commitment to free intellectual inquiry. A university provides civil space for such inquiry by its scholars, as well as for investigations by public intellectuals and expert practitioners.

This series, In the National Interest, embodies Monash University's mission to extend knowledge and encourage informed debate about matters of great significance to Australia's future.

Professor Susan Elliott AM
Interim President and Vice-Chancellor,
Monash University

KIM CORNISH
THE POST-PANDEMIC CHILD

MONASH
UNIVERSITY
PUBLISHING

Monash University Publishing
Matheson Library Annexe
40 Exhibition Walk
Monash University
Clayton, Victoria 3800, Australia
https://publishing.monash.edu

Monash University Publishing brings to the world publications which advance the best traditions of humane and enlightened thought.

ISBN: 9781922979261 (paperback)
ISBN: 9781922979285 (ebook)

Series: In the National Interest
Editor: Greg Bain
Project manager & copyeditor: Paul Smitz
Designer: Peter Long
Typesetter: Cannon Typesetting
Proofreader: Gillian Armitage
Printed in Australia by Ligare Book Printers

A catalogue record for this book is available from the National Library of Australia.

AUTHOR'S NOTE

As someone who is not part of the Aboriginal or Torres Strait Islander community, I am ill-equipped to properly represent how COVID-19 and the current landscape in Australia continue to impact Aboriginal and Torres Strait Islander children. However, I feel it would be remiss not to include First Nations children in a book focusing on the physical and mental health of children in Australia during and after the pandemic. To do this topic any kind of justice, I have leant on the much more qualified knowledge of our Aboriginal and Torres Strait Islander health services and their reports throughout the last few years. I also hope this makes more people aware of these services and the amazing work they do.

Also, throughout this book I have included case studies derived from testimonies that myself and my team have collected, summarised and—to protect the interviewees—de-identified. These case studies are intended to provide essential context through individuals' real-world experiences.

THE POST-PANDEMIC CHILD

The first memories of so many Australian children are typically of activities such as playing at a beach, swimming with friends, eating ice cream on a really hot summer day, and going to school. With just over 2.2 million children going to primary school across six states and two territories, Australia provides a safe place for kids to learn, live and grow. A national pastime for children everywhere is outdoor play, with opportunities to learn new hobbies and make new friends.

Children officially start school after their fifth birthday and complete their primary education at age twelve. These school years are absolutely pivotal in order for a child to thrive. Classroom learning provides a forum for the development of basic reading and number skills, play begins to transform from social pretend play to taking turns in group activities, and learning to socially connect with peers forms critical relationships that will last throughout the childhood years. Access to free schooling and leisure facilities levels the playing field for children from all backgrounds and cultures, allowing them to study and play together irrespective of their circumstances. This Australian way of life helps children to flourish, meet their potential and enjoy their childhood.

In 2019, the world was readying itself for a new decade. There were no major threats to the Australian economy, and families could travel interstate seamlessly, visiting family members no matter where they lived. Australia is fortunate to have one of the world's best healthcare systems, free to all, with child health a priority for all state, territory and federal governments. Children and their families can access specialist services that include a burgeoning mental health service. This is critical given that some children, even those as young as five, can present with challenging behaviours, including physically hurting other children, refusing to leave the house and go to school, and excessive tantrums such as screaming when things don't go their way. These behaviours, if left untreated, rarely completely go away and can escalate as the child grows.

However, although Australia prides itself on its ability to provide essential services and equal opportunities for all, it is impossible to ensure that every child develops optimally in every possible way.

Children are extremely dependent on others, usually their caregivers, to meet their most basic needs, including safe housing, access to nutritious food and clean water, education, health care and emotional support. So those who don't have reliable, stable access to these basic needs are especially vulnerable.

Vulnerability is the term used to describe populations who are at risk of poor outcomes. In regards to childhood, this often refers to poor developmental outcomes that reduce a child's ability to learn at school and make friends, and which put them at risk of later experiencing psychological issues such as refusing to go to school, excessive worry, and acting out aggressive behaviours such as shouting and hitting others. Vulnerable children include those who live in violent or disruptive households; who do not have the digital literacy to access all education resources; or who live in poverty, lacking the financial means to obtain basic necessities. Children with developmental delays that impair the advancement of learning and social skills are also at risk of being left behind. For this group of children, access to service provision in the form of behaviour therapists, classroom aides, transport to school and back, and physical therapy, is essential if they are to feel part of an inclusive environment.

Aboriginal and Torres Strait Islanders, who make up roughly 6 per cent of all Australian children, confront many challenges. This population has a holistic view of good health, with physical, social, emotional, cultural and spiritual wellbeing all contributing to it. But Aboriginal and Torres Strait Islander people face barriers to accessing health services, including a lack of availability, particularly if they live in remote areas, and a lack of culturally appropriate and safe services. This limited access to often basic health assistance can marginalise this population, contributing to a lower standard of health, perpetuating social inequality, and putting the wellbeing of children in these communities at risk.

Other issues were affecting our kids in 2019. To help children grow and flourish, Australian experts in sleep, nutrition and exercise have advocated daily guidelines for children in the primary school years. The National Sleep Foundation recommended in 2015 that children between the ages of five and twelve should sleep uninterrupted for between nine and eleven hours a night.[1] A 2019 report identified that the majority of Australian children meet these requirements, but that as children get older, the proportion not meeting the minimum sleep time increases.[2] In recent years, excessive screen time has been identified as being harmful for children by reducing social interactions with friends and family, and interrupting sleep or preventing its onset. It is recommended that children spend no more than two hours using a screen for entertainment purposes each day, but a 2016 report by the Australian Institute of Family Studies found that a majority of children are exceeding this limit.[3] In particular, 60 per cent of screen time is made up of TV viewing, and the incidence of electronic gaming was found to have more than doubled between the ages of six and eleven.

This increase in technology and screen time has also jeopardised the time children spend exercising. The Australian Department of Health and Aged Care recommends that children engage in at least one hour of varying levels of physical activity every day, with limited sedentary periods.[4] And yet, despite the abundance of wide open spaces and array of physical activity facilities around the country, in 2012 less than one-quarter of Australian children actually met these guidelines.[5] Alarmingly, only one in ten met both the exercise and screen time recommendations.

This profile of Australian kids sketches outcomes both good and bad. But one thing all of these children had in common was that they were living in the pre-pandemic era. Words and phrases like 'social distancing', 'lockdown' and 'online learning' meant nothing to them. Neither they nor their families had any idea of the disruption and the additional challenges to come in 2020—challenges that, three years later, are ongoing for many, and which must be dealt with to safeguard our children's individual and collective futures.

THE PANDEMIC CHILD

The beginning of 2020 was a time of unprecedented devastation and fear in Australia. Two life-changing crises, occurring only a few months apart—the catastrophic Black Summer bushfires and the COVID-19 pandemic—created a wave of turmoil that left a nation reeling.

Across the summer of 2019–20, bushfires ravaged vast tracts of land, particularly in south-eastern Australia. Thousands of homes were destroyed, while thirty-four people and several billion animals were killed. Both indirectly and directly, the blazes are thought to have impacted around 80 per cent of the Australian population. Among the most severely affected were Indigenous communities in New South Wales and Victoria. One in ten infants and children affected by the fires were Indigenous Australians.[6] Not only did many First Nations people lose their homes and land, they also reportedly suffered racism as well as neglect due to some federal and state disaster-management plans that did not specifically address the unique needs of Indigenous populations.[7]

The scale of psychological distress experienced by children during the fires—symptoms of depression, anxiety, fearfulness and post-traumatic stress—especially those from more vulnerable backgrounds, was enormous. A report published by the

Australian National University in 2022 found that, twelve to eighteen months after Black Summer ended, parents with children impacted by the fires reported more behavioural and emotional challenges than the parents of children in unaffected communities.[8] Children in close proximity to the bushfires suffered from both physical and mental health issues, including lung problems from the inhalation of smoke, and symptoms of anxiety and depression, such as poor sleep and excessive worry.

The media coverage of the devastation, including the loss of human lives and wildlife, itself contributed to the potential development of mental health problems. Exposure to distressing news events is upsetting for young children, even if they don't clearly understand what is happening. They may be scared by what they see, worried about their family's safety, or overwhelmed by continuous reporting of negative events—kids may even think the same disaster is happening multiple times. This can manifest in children becoming worried, anxious, having trouble sleeping, or acting out, particularly if the media coverage also upsets their caregivers.

But just months into Australia's recovery from the megafire, the nation would be thrown the biggest curveball in its recent history. The first report of the coronavirus, an infectious disease often resulting in moderate respiratory illness, occurred in December

2019 in Wuhan, China. Then, on 25 January 2020, the first case of COVID-19 in Australia was confirmed after an infected man returned from Wuhan. By the end of the month, the World Health Organization (WHO) had declared the virus a public health emergency. Australia recorded its first death from the virus on 1 March, and COVID-19 was officially classified as a pandemic on 11 March. A few days later, the Victorian Government cancelled the Formula 1 Grand Prix just hours before the event, creating a sense of uncertainty, unease and shock around the state, and providing a taste of what was to come. By 20 March, Australia had closed its borders to all non-residents, and a week later, all incoming residents had to spend two weeks isolating in 'quarantine hotels'. At the same time, social distancing rules were enforced as state governments began to close all 'non-essential' services, including restaurants and clubs. Individual states began to shut themselves off from the rest of the nation as case numbers grew.

What followed were two years of uncertainty in Australia, encompassing various lockdowns and sundry restrictions. Some places fared better than others. Melbourne became regarded as the world's most locked-down city, enduring 263 days of strict shutdowns. Mid-2020 saw the start of mask wearing in an effort to reduce the spread of the virus, and Victoria announced tough measures such as an overnight curfew and limiting the movements of residents to within a 5-kilometre radius of their homes. By the end of 2020, 28 408 cases of COVID-19 had been confirmed in Australia, with 909 deaths. The country's initial response to the virus was envied by many other nations that had experienced accelerated rates of cases, with various experts praising Australia for its containment of the virus. Few people, if anyone, could have anticipated what 2021 had in store for the nation.

The start of the second year of the pandemic saw the first doses of a COVID-19 vaccine being administered. As vaccines were rolled out across the country, some people began to feel hopeful about a return to normality. Certainly in Victoria, the drugs created some light at the end of the lockdown tunnel—it was only when 70 per cent of those aged over sixteen years had received two doses of a COVID-19 vaccine that residents would be free to venture further afield than their 5-kilometre zone. By Christmas 2021, 92.7 per cent of Victorians over twelve years of age had received two vaccine doses, and most families were able to spend the holidays together. The health situation was still dire, however: on Christmas day, over 60 000 Australians had confirmed active cases of the virus, more than double what the country had experienced over the entirety of the previous year. Between Christmas and the new year, another 100 000 Australians were included in the count, bringing the total to over 395 000 cases and 2239 deaths. It was not the end to 2021 that people were expecting.

Despite daily case numbers remaining in the tens of thousands throughout 2022, that year saw the beginning of what was termed 'COVID normal'. Travel restrictions began to lift across the country— after 697 days of a hard border, Western Australia reopened itself to the rest of Australia and the world. Students were once again populating classrooms, sporting clubs were open, and children were now able to freely play outdoors and with each other. While the worry of contracting the virus still permeated society, reduced isolation rules for infected individuals and other eased restrictions meant we could begin to freely go about our daily lives again. In this sense, 2022 marked the end of lockdowns and the return to school of what can be called the 'post-pandemic child'. Finally, in May 2023, WHO declared that COVID-19 was no longer officially a global health pandemic.

This recap is necessary because to understand the needs of today's child—the post-pandemic child— we first need to put a spotlight on Australian children as they endured the pandemic. For over two million schoolchildren under the age of ten years, the pandemic drastically altered their lives. The sudden jolt out of routine and structured activities made them particularly vulnerable to the psychological fallout of the pandemic. Seemingly overnight, key challenges emerged as families were thrown into online schooling, severe restrictions were placed on social gatherings, and changing family structures saw parents, carers and children cohabiting 24/7 with significantly reduced opportunities for structured sport and other outside play. There was an increase in screen time that coincided with reduced physical activity, and children became more isolated, and worried about contracting and spreading the virus. The pandemic also sparked an increase in vulnerable children through a rise in domestic violence, caregivers struggling to make ends meet as they lost jobs, growing developmental and learning difficulties, and cultural challenges. Every day, families were left questioning what tomorrow would look like.

Life Far from Normal

By April 2020, Australia was in widespread lockdown and schools were online only. Families faced restrictions in movement, including time-limited outdoor exercise, the termination of social or group gatherings, and the closure of businesses and public institutions. Alarmist social media and news sources further compounded the feelings of uncertainty and fear. Children were daily exposed to case numbers and death tolls as media platforms constantly reported on the crisis. The news sites were endeavouring to update the community, but this type of exposure can cause intense fear, increased stress and even panic attacks in children.

In the context of these disruptions to normal life, the mental health and wellbeing of children began to be a significant concern for communities and governments. In those early days, of course, there was sparse research data to inform decision-makers and governments, limiting their ability to directly address the key needs of Australian children, particularly those from the most vulnerable communities; for example, families in low-socioeconomic-status areas. And so, without enough early detection, and due to a lack of timely intervention, pandemic-related mental health issues soon began to significantly impact the learning and behaviours of children at home. The most immediate concerns reported by parents stemmed from the sudden and prolonged isolation, which created anxiety and stress in children who were only just beginning to build friendships and form social connections with their peers. As we moved into the second, third and fourth months of lockdown measures, these clusters of risk behaviours were only exacerbated, causing an already overburdened child service sector to buckle. Spotlighting a single four-month period, between January and April 2020, Kids Helpline responded to 12 per cent more counselling contacts compared with the same period in 2019.

No School, No Play Today

Every experience we have teaches us something, and for children, so many experiences are brand new. When lockdown measures closed schools, community centres and aged-care homes, children could no longer connect to families and friends outside of a screen. This suddenly altered when and how they developed their first set of social skills, impacting their ability to make friends and learn about cooperation and sharing—they were simply no longer able to spend time with other children, sharing toys and playing games together. Also, with lockdowns interrupting children's opportunities to interact with both adults and children, they were not able to develop the basic communication skills needed to socialise, impairing their ability to interact with others when they eventually did return to school.

The impact of all this isolation was immediate, unprecedented and pervasive. Being 'locked in' with their households created new social dynamics and tensions for these kids. Some families grew closer, strengthening their bonds and creating new traditions, while others saw a rise in conflict and aggression between parents and children. Everyday social lives were put on pause—children missed out on play dates, swimming lessons, birthdays, sleepovers, visits to grandparents, and so much more. But equally, the dynamics within the family changed, with parents often having to take on a new role as 'teacher' within a virtual school context. This occurred irrespective of work responsibilities, family income, and the available space and resources. It presented an unequal playing field that allowed some children to thrive, while others just survived.

'Glenda', a mother of three, found the experience of eliminating all extracurricular activities very difficult. Prior to the pandemic, she'd lived a busy and social life, seeing friends and family, attending a play group, and going on fun outings with her children. Missing out on these experiences left her and her family feeling tense and exhausted. Going for a walk around the block became the highlight of the day—her children greatly missed their friends, sports activities and playing in the park.

Outdoor play is a quintessential part of an Australian childhood. Many of us treasure memories of backyard barbecues, games of cricket, netball or footy, and trips to the beach. Grazed knees and dirty shirts were the evidence that we were building the foundations of our own identity and the confidence to explore our environment. These moments helped us to form social relationships that would be continuously built upon during the critical formative years of childhood and beyond. In 2020, however, most children were confined to playing inside the family home; if there was outdoor play, it was limited to self-play or with household members only.

In some parts of Victoria and New South Wales, these restrictions even extended to the closure of playgrounds. Often, a barricade of thick tape surrounded playground equipment, visually alerting children that it was not safe to play there. This took away options for families without backyards or limited access to community spaces. Many families were further hampered in accessing outdoor recreational areas by the introduction of 'zones' outside of which they could not go, except for a strict shortlist of urgent reasons. Children in apartment buildings, or otherwise in built-up or inner-city areas, often shared a handful of play spaces with hundreds of other families that they were not allowed to interact with, culminating in fear and a hesitancy to play with other children, even as restrictions began to ease.

We know that physical activity is critical to our mental health and wellbeing, and this is obviously as true for children as it is for adults. Research has highlighted the added benefit of exercising in social settings, especially the formation of relationships in a focused and collegial environment that promotes self-confidence, independence and teamwork.

'Kai', a mother of seven, lived in a public housing block in Melbourne's inner north. In July 2020, residents in the neighbouring apartment complex were allowed to leave their homes to exercise or shop, and they could stand on their balconies to get fresh air and play, but for Kai and her children, life was very different. For five days, her building was placed under a strict, hard lockdown: no-one was allowed to leave their apartment for any reason. The residents weren't even given proper notice, meaning Kai had limited food in her fridge; even when she was brought a 'food package', it didn't contain enough servings for all her children. More than 500 police surrounded Kai's building, so residents could only access fresh air through their windows. Outdoor play was now illegal for Kai's children, who were stuck indoors.

For the people residing in the public housing complex, the majority of whom were culturally and linguistically diverse, this hard lockdown brought psychological and emotional trauma. Needless to say, the effects on a child can be longlasting.

Children with 'Square Eyes'

As a result of schools closing and social activities ceasing, screen time became the only way for children to socialise, learn and relax. In the rush to adapt, government and educators naively assumed that all children would have access to the necessary digital technologies; however, it would soon become clear that this was not the case.

Prior to the pandemic, the national guidelines for children outlined the importance of no more than two hours of sedentary screen time each day, excluding schoolwork. Exceeding this recommendation can have both physical and mental health implications, including behavioural problems, attention issues and lower self-esteem. But during the COVID-19 lockdowns, Australian children's screen time rose by a huge 50 per cent, with some children spending up to twenty-seven more hours a week than usual looking at screens. It was clear that, in the midst of lockdowns and isolation, the national guidelines were simply not achievable. However, experts struggled to suggest new guidelines for device use for online schooling periods. For school-aged children, the guidelines depended on the child's lifestyle, and they emphasised what the child was doing on the device rather than how long they were using it for. Ultimately, it was left to parents to monitor the quality and content of screen time—as well as simultaneously engage with their children, and ensure the appropriate resources were being accessed, all while keeping up with their own work and responsibilities. For many families, this advice was impractical and unrealistic to implement.

A key concern now surrounds the issue of lockdown screen time potentially having become the norm for many children, with some as young as five years old having developed an educational and emotional reliance on technology. This increased use has inevitably resulted in poorer social connections and social development, with screen-induced tantrums having become the norm in some households when parents try to encourage technology-free hobbies or activities.

'Mary', the parent of a six-year old child, struggled during the pandemic to get her son motivated to exercise rather than 'resorting to screens'. It was particularly challenging to find opportunities for him to socialise, play and learn without requiring a screen. In fact, Mary's child found that the best part of being at home during lockdown was 'going on [his] iPad'.

Anxiety and Isolation

The fear of COVID-19 had a huge impact on young children's mental health during 2020. They expressed worry and anxiety not just for themselves but even more so for family members—in particular for grandparents, parents, uncles, aunts and friends who might die if they caught COVID. They also expressed fear about the risks facing parents and relatives who worked in vulnerable areas of service, such as hospitals and supermarkets. These concerns were only made worse by the barrage of endless fear-mongering and horror stories presented on the news and in popular media. The effect was deepened by official government communications focused on COVID-19 infections and deaths, information that parents and families watched daily in an attempt to better understand their uncertain futures. Epidemiology experts shared concerns that children were likely to act as carriers of COVID-19, suggesting that they posed a greater risk when it came to others getting sick. This led children to worry about spreading any infection they might pick up, and feeling that they could be responsible for their family becoming very sick. In some children, this led to abnormally high anxiety levels that manifested in nightmares, obsessive-compulsive behaviours such as continuous handwashing, and guilt. In the eyes of young children, the world had become an unsafe place. As one teacher noted, the five-year-olds were not like five-year-olds, but instead carried unseen burdens of worry and responsibility, forced to 'grow up' too soon.

For older children, their worries were centred on their families too, and also on other relationships. They were left asking: Can we afford everything we usually have? Will my parents lose their jobs? Are my parents fighting because of me? How can I make my parents happy again? When will schools reopen and I can see my friends? Will I get to have a birthday party? Will I ever see my primary school again? How will I make friends in high school? Meanwhile, for children who already had an existing mental health diagnosis, the fear of getting COVID-19 and the associated restrictions triggered an escalation of symptoms and behaviours that for some became debilitating, including sleep issues and extreme worry resulting in avoidance behaviours.

One older child, 'Jade', suffers from obsessive-compulsive disorder (OCD) that was exacerbated by the pandemic, specifically the need to stay 'clean'. Prior to COVID-19, Jade had displayed various behaviours and traits of OCD, such as constantly washing her hands and refusing to go to places she viewed as 'dirty', like shopping centres and supermarkets. Then, during the pandemic, hearing constant messages about needing to self-sanitise and keep everything germ-free, Jade's thinking and behaviours spiralled. She viewed everything outside of her home as infectious and washed her hands so frequently that she developed a skin condition. Her behaviour began to tear her family apart. There was tension and aggression between Jade and her brother, who she viewed as 'germy'. She refused to spend time with her family—she would not even eat in the same room as them. She isolated herself in her room, believing that it was the only place safe from germs.

Isolation more broadly greatly exacerbated children's anxiety. In March 2020, the Australian Government imposed nationwide rules, including lockdown measures, to help prevent the spread of COVID-19. These measures rapidly led to the closure of Australia's borders to the outside world, and the eventual separation of states and territories which began to enforce their own rules and restrictions. In this fight against the spread of COVID-19, the first state to isolate was Victoria.

For families living in Melbourne, it all began with forty-three days of restrictions from March, and by mid-2020 Victorian residents were all too familiar with the phrase 'only four reasons to leave home', enduring for 111 more days some of the strictest lockdowns worldwide. Towards the end of the year, with the easing of restrictions for holiday celebrations, families didn't yet know that in 2021, they would experience another 108 days in lockdown. Over these two years, children missed out on in-person teaching and seeing their friends for roughly thirty-five weeks—just five weeks shy of a full school year.

Victoria's—specifically, Melbourne's—level of restrictions were not the envy of other Australian cities. Many states put in place laws preventing Victorians from travelling across their borders, to not allow what was happening in Victoria to spread across the country. This effectively made Victoria a pariah state, an example of a worst-case scenario. Even as Victorians began to see an easing of restrictions, they still faced weeks-long snap lockdowns, with only a few hours' warning. This uncertainty meant that even when freedoms began to be restored, families remained afraid these freedoms could disappear the very next day. For young Victorians, this period conditioned a deep sense of uncertainty and fear about the future, including not knowing when they would return to school and if their family members would catch the virus. Meanwhile, children in most other states remained in the classroom and enjoyed face-to-face teaching, organised sports activities and social gatherings, albeit with some rules such as the wearing of face masks and handwashing.

'Sharon', a mother of two in Melbourne's south-eastern suburbs, recounted the feeling of completely losing track of time. The ongoing nature of Victoria's lockdowns left her feeling fatigued, forgetting to eat, and struggling to stay on top of work and monitoring online schooling. In particular, she was concerned for her ten-year-old son, who had autism. Despite attending therapy for years and making huge progress, stay-at-home orders brought back old behaviours. Worry about her son regressing in his treatment, combined with the stresses of managing a household while working from home, and trying to raise two children, were all compounded in the extended lockdowns.

In This Together?

Not only were the experiences of children different across states and territories, they were also different across postcodes. The popular catchphrase 'We're all in this together' no longer rang true. Instead, it presented a false sense of solidarity. We were not all in this together. We were separated by factors such as socioeconomic challenges, employment, health, access to space and resources, the complex dynamics of family relationships, and safety within homes. Vulnerable children across these domains, those who could not access basic necessities, were disproportionately affected.

'Olivia' was eight years old when the pandemic hit. She settled into online schooling quickly, using her own laptop to attend classes and complete her class work. After school, she would often go for a walk with her parents and brother to the local park where she would inevitably run into some school friends. On the weekends, she would play in her backyard with her brother, usually on their trampoline.

But this was not the lived experience of all children. An education expert, 'Professor Black', discussed how, when COVID-19 first hit, a whole new wave of educationally disadvantaged families appeared. There was an increase in the number of families struggling to obtain the basic needs of shelter and food, but also families who had to balance working and online schooling, looking after multiple children, and managing children's weakened emotional well-being. The reality of playing in backyards, spending time with family and completing school work on one's own laptop was not attainable by all.

Children Experiencing Digital Inequality

It's often assumed that every child has access to the internet, that every family has access to multiple digital tools including iPads and laptops. By this assumption, all children should have been able to connect and learn throughout the pandemic regardless of location and financial circumstances. However, it quickly became clear that this assumption did not hold true. Children who came from economically disadvantaged families, lived in regional or remote areas, or experienced a disability or learning difficulty, became increasingly isolated and, in educational terms, left behind. The Australian Digital Inclusion Index, used to identify those who are likely to have limited access to digital technology, found that in 2021 up to a quarter of Australians experienced digital exclusion.[9]

A lack of digital literacy, technology access and reliable internet all impact a child's ability to navigate an online education and stay engaged with their schooling. During the pandemic, children experiencing the digital divide were unable to keep up social connections and develop friendships from home like their digitally equipped peers, making the eventual return to school even more daunting. Fortunately, help became available for many. Communities, businesses and not-for-profit organisations came together to provide internet access and laptops to struggling students, and state governments gave thousands of laptops and wi-fi dongles to schools to distribute to those in need. Millions of dollars were also invested in helping disadvantaged schools educate their students.

Prior to COVID-19, 'Oscar' and his single mother would spend their time at local shopping centres and libraries to access free wi-fi. But after saving up for a laptop for Oscar's school work, the family could not afford an internet connection at home. When the pandemic hit and libraries and malls closed, Oscar, like many other children living in poverty, could not access online classes. Despite the fact that he loved his schooling, he was now destined to fall behind his digitally included peers.

Children in Poverty

We use phrases such as 'poverty' and 'the breadline' to describe what we deem the lowest level of income a family can earn and still maintain an acceptable standard of living. In 2020, the Melbourne Institute of Applied Economic and Social Research updated the poverty line for a two-adult, two-child family, with only one adult working, to $1054.12 a week, inclusive of housing costs. At that time, going by this new threshold, one in six Australian children—roughly 760 000 kids—were classified as living in poverty.[10] These children experienced increased worry and other stresses associated with where their next meal would come from, whether parents and guardians would keep their jobs and make enough money for the family to survive, whether they would keep their home, and the very real risk of losing the necessary technological equipment, with little or no ability to replace anything if it broke. For both parents and children, life and stability seemed to be balancing on a fine edge, only one slip away from disaster.

For those children with parents who could not work from home and were away for long work hours, trying to earn enough to get by on, this also meant they became the caregivers and unpaid babysitters of younger siblings. It is not uncommon in lower-income households, or households with certain cultural back-grounds and belief systems, to expect older children to monitor, teach and care for their younger brothers and sisters. This does not always mean teenagers or young adults, as children as young as eight years old have taken on some carer responsibilities. In-person schooling provided such children with brief opportu-nities to be free of these extra responsibilities and to focus on their own lives and learning. The removal of this meant some children could no longer escape the demands of home life. They were expected to take on the roles of carer and guardian at the expense of their own childhood.

The situation was not any easier for families where parents were not working the same hours as they had previously. During the pandemic, more than a quarter of Australian households experienced job or income loss, and 28 per cent had difficulty paying for food.[11] A well-established connection exists between children in families experiencing financial adversity and poor child mental health—it is simply unrealistic to assume that children don't notice or aren't aware that their parents are struggling to get by. Parents and children who experienced economic hardship during COVID-19 reported high levels of mental health symptoms and emphasised the struggle to cope with everyday life. Government financial initiatives became an important factor in maintaining mental health and wellbeing for these families.

'Joyce' is the grandmother and legal guardian of her six-year-old granddaughter. During the pandemic, financial difficulties saw the family living without a computer and hardly any internet access. Joyce's granddaughter had to complete online schooling on her grandmother's mobile phone, often running out of mobile data before having completed all the work or uploading assignments. Due to poverty, this girl was set to miss out on vital learning opportunities that most take for granted.

Children in Unsafe Households

Stay-at-home orders exponentially increased the time children were spending with potentially harmful and violent caregivers. Even prior to the arrival of COVID-19, domestic and family violence was seen as a global epidemic, with women and girls disproportionately impacted. During the pandemic, harsh lockdowns and isolation only increased the volatility in vulnerable households, placing families in really dangerous situations. Due to movement restrictions, women could no longer file interventions against violent partners in person and instead had to use the internet, adding further stress and the fear of being monitored. In a matter of weeks after the beginning of the first lockdown of 2020, referrals for children's counselling went through the roof.

Where school once offered a respite, an escape from violent home lives, children were now trapped, with no trained eyes looking out for their wellbeing. Although child-protection services operated throughout the pandemic, they witnessed a significant drop in the number of reported cases of potential child abuse by teachers, family members and neighbours. Telehealth services, practically the only option for children to report abuse, stagnated as children declined to use them, from fear of being overheard. In the absence of a safe and secure means of getting help, children who did try and seek assistance reported extremely high levels of stress, anxiety and fear, including thoughts of suicide, largely driven by emotional abuse and isolation in confined living spaces.

Recognising the urgent need to act and respond to this growing crisis, both state and federal governments pledged immediate support. This included funding for alternative accommodation, household-related expenses, basic needs, and access to Kids Helpline and Beyond Blue. And so, throughout the lockdown, a number of women and children living in violent households were able to leave, regardless of restrictions, to find safe accommodation.

'Holly' is a child protection officer who saw her caseload drop significantly during the pandemic. She tried to speak to clients over the phone but was frequently met with resistance or a call suddenly terminating. She tried Zoom calls but poor internet connections often made these impossible. Because there was no opportunity for safe planning with teachers and medical professionals, Holly saw an increase in emergency calls to police and families seeking refuge.

Children with Developmental and Learning Disadvantages

In 2021, 22 per cent of Australian children started school with a developmental vulnerability, the most common being attention deficit hyperactivity disorder (ADHD), dyslexia, autism spectrum disorder (ASD) and intellectual disability (ID).[12] These children were especially vulnerable during the pandemic due to changes in daily routines, service provision such as transport to school, and service delivery— from in-person services through to telehealth appointments to accommodate social distancing. The suddenness of the changes was debilitating for so many children, causing tremendous strain on their families, including siblings. Parents reported increased mental health issues such as depression and anxiety, and elevated levels of stress and frustration, with the COVID restrictions prompting a rise in behavioural problems in many children with developmental delays. For example, children with ADHD, which is characterised by hyperactivity and/or inattention, reported high levels of sadness, depression and loneliness. Compared to before the pandemic, they also exercised less, spent more time on screens and found less enjoyment in everyday activities. There were also greater barriers to accessing health care, particularly ADHD medication.

'Andrea' is a mother of two children, one of whom has ADHD. Remote learning saw her children struggling to complete work without the usual classroom structure and a teacher directing them. There were concerns that their education and academic potential would be overlooked because online learning delivery did not fit their learning needs.

For children with ASD, a developmental disorder that impairs communication and interactions, the loss of a school routine was a huge source of anxiety. Their parents were very concerned about losing institutional support from schools and missing out on social interactions. Similarly, for children with ID who struggle to learn and function at the expected level in everyday life, the lockdowns reduced access to much-needed educational and therapy services. Parents struggled to explain what COVID-19 was, and why it wasn't possible to leave the house, in a way their children could understand, leading to uncertainty and anxiety. Lockdowns seemed to accentuate already high levels of emotional and behavioural problems in children with ID, and their parents experienced even lower levels of wellbeing. The pandemic reduced access to social, educational and emotional support, leaving parents struggling to help their kids.

'Sally' is a mother of three whose eldest child is on the autism spectrum. She recounted the huge impact of the pandemic on her eldest's behaviour and mood, and highlighted how this burdened the whole family. For Sally, being confined indoors with three children was incredibly difficult, especially having to always think about her eldest's needs and how their behaviour could affect her other children.

Children from Culturally Diverse Communities

For families from non-English-speaking countries or who did not speak English at home, understanding COVID-19 restrictions and why they were necessary caused a great deal of stress. In communities across Australia, families were often left without government information written in their home language and were dependent on religious leaders to provide critical COVID-19 updates. This heightened fears for the physical and financial safety of their families. Refugees, in particular, were more likely to live in community housing not suitable for extended periods of isolation, and to be employed in high-exposure essential services. As the pandemic progressed, it became harder to seek support from cultural and social groups or financial services. Families on temporary visas, including asylum seekers, were excluded from some forms of government support in Australia—despite losing work and income as was happening to Australian citizens, they could not access the same financial support, reducing their children's ability to learn and grow. For children from non-English-speaking backgrounds, the shift to online schooling and largely self-directed work caused many to struggle, and the broader challenges that accompanied COVID-19 led to worsening mental health and wellbeing. Limited access to digital technology and the internet also impeded learning opportunities.

Seven years before COVID-19 hit, 'Lakshitha' came to Australia with her family, including her infant child, seeking asylum from Sri Lanka. Despite having working rights, it was difficult for Lakshitha and her husband to find employment, and they struggled to support their three children. The pandemic brought more job insecurity and financial strain, forcing them to borrow money from friends, as they had no savings or superannuation and were not eligible for Centrelink support. Their local church community stepped in to provide them with food packages. Lakshitha's family was just one of many in the asylum-seeker cohort who faced extreme financial hardship due to COVID-19.

Aboriginal and Torres Strait Islander Children

Prior to the pandemic, researchers emphasised that Aboriginal and Torres Strait Islander communities face many barriers to accessing health care, such as a lack of services in remote areas and a dearth of culturally appropriate physical and mental health options. Policymakers refer to this push to improve the currently insufficient health care for First Nations communities as 'bridging the gap'. Australian Bureau of Statistics data from 2008 for First Nations people highlight mental health, cardiovascular disease, injury and cancer as just some of the health concerns that disproportionately impact Indigenous communities. The addition of a global pandemic to this chronic and ongoing lack of appropriate resources made access to vital health care even more difficult.

An acute and sudden switch from in-person to remote health services was difficult for many Australians, but none more so than the 100 000 First Nations families identified in the 2021 Census as living in remote areas or experiencing socioeconomic disadvantage and cost-of-living pressures. Those who could access technology for communication found it was not enough to escape feelings of isolation, but for many, this wasn't even an option. The National Indigenous Australians Agency has outlined how the pandemic highlighted the digital divide that restricts Aboriginal and Torres Strait Islander families from accessing the same resources as other communities around the country.

The Secretariat of National Aboriginal and Islander Child Care (SNAICC) asserts that raising a child is a collective responsibility, with extended family playing a critical role in the upbringing of youth. To be separated from family is to be separated from community and Country, undermining an individual's sense of self and resilience, and so the inability during the pandemic to meet these fundamental needs of connection only added to the impact of COVID-19 measures on Indigenous mental health. The pandemic created a disconnection between family, community and culture, with families not being able to support each other, participate in cultural practices or return to Country, to the detriment to their social and mental wellbeing.

Indigenous parents commonly reported that their children experienced fear and worry, with pre-existing anxieties exacerbated during lockdowns as inadequate access to support services coincided with cultural and social disconnection. And yet, despite all this adversity, Aboriginal communities and organisations, like SNAICC, came together, more than ever before, to keep people safe and show their support. In the face of cancellations of community events and gatherings, families tried to maintain their sense of self and ensure their children were able to obtain a comprehensive cultural education and connection.

Children in the Midst of Disaster

'Sam', his wife and child experienced first-hand the Black Summer bushfires on the NSW South Coast. This major life event caused endless worry for the young family, and the arrival of COVID-19 so soon after the fires only compounded their stress. They were still concerned about the impact of extremely high levels of pollution on their health when the new crisis hit. However, Sam noted that his family's resilience and closeness helped them to navigate these extremely tough circumstances.

The declaration of a global pandemic just months after the loss of homes and lives in the Black Summer catastrophe meant many families were propelled into a second major disaster without having had the chance to overcome the first. With the announcement of lock-downs, many families were left wondering how they could stay at home when they had no home to stay at. Multiple lifetime traumas happening just months apart are incredibly difficult to manage. The cumulative effects of consecutive disasters often puts the mental health, wellbeing and physical health of those affected in jeopardy. Bushfire-affected communities were thrown into another state of devastation, potentially without access to their usual primary-care services and social circles—and in the most severe cases, without their belongings or income. The disruptions stemming from both events also impacted children's ability to go outside, see friends and attend school.

Bushfires were not the only natural disaster to ravage parts of Australia around that time. In both 2021 and 2022, extreme rainfall resulted in widespread flooding on the east coast of Australia. In March 2021, towns around New South Wales experienced their worst flooding in over sixty years. More than 18 000 residents were forced to evacuate; the NSW State

Emergency Service responded to 12 000 requests, and 1000 people were rescued. The east coast became a natural disaster zone, with homes submerged, businesses and schools destroyed, and possessions lost, exposing families to even more uncertainty.

The paramount effects of multiple events on the wellbeing of children are devastating. They experience a rise in trauma, mental health problems and family violence. For those already enduring economic hardship or social disadvantage, the effects are magnified even more. Despite the resilience of many children and young people, some experience post-traumatic stress disorder, anxiety and depression. This can leave deep mental scars. In addition, other elements of disasters, such as amplified media coverage of traumatic events and exposure to familial distress, can further increase and sustain negative impacts on children's education and health. And so it was the case that, during the pandemic, vulnerable children who'd experienced the bushfires or floods were at risk of being more adversely affected than peers who did not undergo the trauma of these natural disasters.

THE POST-PANDEMIC CHILD

At the time of writing, it has been three years since the everyday lives of Australian children and their families were forever changed by the advent of the pandemic. Fortunately, children proved less likely to become critically ill from a COVID-19 infection compared with adults. Nonetheless, the indirect effects of the lockdowns and other restrictions have had profound, wide-ranging and longlasting effects, including prolonged mental health problems, a reluctance to play or socialise outside the home, and the highest rate of school refusal seen in a generation. Many children still do not feel safe enough to amuse themselves in playgrounds, visit friends' homes or learn with other kids in a classroom. The habits and lifestyle patterns formed in the pandemic will take time to unlearn. We need to be patient, but we cannot sit back and do nothing.

In focusing on the issues our children now face, we invariably turn to the lasting legacy of the pandemic. So what is the state of play for Australian children? And what are our responsibilities as a nation when it comes to helping them thrive?

Re-entering the Classroom

In late 2021, we took our first tentative steps out of the COVID bubble, and life for many of us began to include some semblance of our old daily school and work routines. But two years of uncertainty and restrictions had left their mark. In such a short period of time, the world as we knew it had changed drastically.

'Jeff' is the grandfather of an eight-year-old girl. At the start of 2023 he dropped his granddaughter off at her Year 2 classroom and was astonished to see all of the children sitting down playing by themselves. They weren't talking to each other; rather, many were occupied on iPads.

For some students, it had been a full two years since they had experienced in-person schooling, and the habits and behaviours forged during lockdown were apparent during the return to face-to-face classes. 'Ms Brown', a primary-school teacher in Melbourne, was excited about classrooms and playgrounds filling with children again. What she didn't anticipate was the rise in difficult student behaviours that she and her colleagues hadn't been trained to deal with. Ms Brown also noted that, post-pandemic, she was spending a lot more time and energy dealing with behaviours she would've expected in much younger children.

For many teachers, the return to classroom teaching has brought with it unexpected levels of disciplinary issues, including an increase in school-ground fighting, children not paying attention, and children deliberately distracting others. This is why promoting positive student behaviour is a key priority for educators in 2023, with many using techniques such as limiting distractions in the classroom, increasing student engagement during lessons, and taking the time to focus on fundamental behavioural skills such as effective communication.

During the lockdowns, data modelling predicted that, as a result of the COVID-19 disruptions, children would end up a year behind where they should be with their learning. This delay in learning would worsen for disadvantaged children who simply did not have access to the tools and environments needed to gain any benefit from remote learning. Bold statements were made in the media claiming that COVID-19 was erasing years of educational gains for students. Let's examine whether this predicted academic downfall has actually been realised in Australian children. Three years after the first lockdown measures were imposed, just how does a post-pandemic child compare academically to the pre-pandemic child?

In terms of measuring academic performance in its most traditional sense, national and age-specific assessment programs such as the National Assessment Program—Literacy and Numeracy (NAPLAN) provide a pre- and post-assessment of five learning domains: reading, writing, spelling, grammar and punctuation, and numeracy. NAPLAN is completed every year by students in years 3, 5, 7 and 9 to measure fundamental skills. The data informs policymakers and education leaders on how Australian students are progressing in their learning. When we compare scores across 2019–22, all five areas saw only a slight decrease in the number of Year 3 students (ages 8–9) who met the minimum standard level of achievement. Similar trends are seen for Year 5 (ages 10–11), Year 7 (ages 12–13) and Year 9 (ages 14–15) students, with some domains even seeing a slight increase in the number of students reaching the minimum threshold. In 2022, experts advised that this slight drop in results is no cause for concern. For the state of Victoria, for example, despite receiving almost a full school year of online learning over two years, children still performed at the same level or higher than all other states and territories around Australia. So in terms of numeracy and literacy, it's not as bad as we first thought.

Why do these results suggest that the education of children has not declined as dramatically as expected? NAPLAN only measures discrete domains which lend themselves to online learning through strict and well-defined learning materials and expectations. Structured testing can only measure the ability of those who show up to take the tests, giving us scores that can be cleaned and averaged to then be generalised for an entire student population. Other important areas of early learning, however, like physical education, music and art, cannot be assessed through highly structured formative testing methods. They require different spaces and resources that were not accessible during the pandemic.

And so, in 2023, educational policymakers have been urging schools to focus on a method of teaching that will facilitate the rebuilding of physical, psychological and social skills alongside the broader curriculum. But this responsibility doesn't just rest with teachers. Children, families and school communities all need to be involved in order to help our students regain the skills that were lost, for socioeconomically advantaged and disadvantaged children alike.

School Refusals

A sharp decline in primary school attendance rates can be seen at the start of 2022, as schools reopened for in-person teaching. Prior to the pandemic, in 2019, 76.4 per cent of Australian students in years 1–6 (ages 6–12) attended at least 90 per cent of school days. When this data was collected post-pandemic, in the first semester of 2022, this number stood at 53 per cent. This drop in attendance is likely due to the ongoing issue of COVID-19 and children staying home when sick. Natural disasters were also occurring, with widespread disruption in Queensland and New South Wales. However, these external disruptions do not fully account for the unprecedented rise of school absenteeism in primary-school children. We have all experienced feeling unmotivated and reluctant to go to school or work. But for many children now, the thought of going to school causes feelings of distress, meaning they will do almost anything to avoid attending. This is referred to as school refusal.

Outside of the impact of COVID-19, school refusal stems from a number of factors, such as social issues and bullying, learning difficulties, family issues, challenges in adjusting to new schools, and mental health issues, such as anxiety and depression. COVID-19 exacerbated these factors and added additional health-related anxieties to the mix. But it differs significantly from other school attendance problems, such as truancy, or the withdrawal of a child from school by their parents so as to put the child on an 'alternate career pathway' or have them take on family responsibilities. In the context of school refusal, it's not that children *won't* go to school, but rather that they *can't* go to school, for emotional and psychological reasons. School refusal is sometimes seen as a phobia, and the emotional distress stemming from this can manifest in physical illness around school time, a refusal to leave the bed or house, or extreme emotional reactions. Persistent school refusal reinforces the ongoing fear and can significantly impact a child's academic and social development, potentially placing them at a great disadvantage to their peers. To put it another way, the longer school refusal persists, the harder it is to help a child return to school.

We currently lack reliable data on the number of school refusals, mostly due to under-reporting or a reluctance to report for fear of repercussions. This leads to the question: did the pandemic exacerbate this issue, or did it just shine a spotlight on it? Given how unreliable measuring school refusal is, it is not clear just how prevalent the issue was in the pre-pandemic child. However, we certainly know the post-pandemic child is experiencing school refusals, as evidenced by specialist referrals, school-indicated data and even parent support groups. A Facebook group for parents and educators of children experiencing school refusal, called School Can't, grew by almost 7000 members from 2019 to 2023. Virtual School Victoria (VSV), based in Melbourne, found that the number of primary school children who took part in its online curriculum due to school refusal doubled between 2018 and 2022—in fact, almost 50 per cent of students at VSV cited school refusal as a reason for enrolling. These children often present with comorbidities such as anxiety and learning difficulties.

'Alice' was one of the students whose school refusal behaviours emerged post-pandemic. At just ten years old, Alice was terrified of spending the day at school, so much so that she experienced panic attacks that sometimes lasted for weeks. Alice's whole family was affected, particularly her mother who had to look after her at home and miss work. Fortunately, Alice's school worked with her to scale back her onsite hours and then gradually increase them until she felt brave enough to spend a whole day at school.

Compounding the problem is the fact that the wait time to see a psychologist has soared, with some specialists receiving over ten new referrals every day and some children waiting over six months to see a professional. And this is just the situation facing vulnerable children in urban areas. For children in rural or remote areas, there is often no psychologist nor a waiting list to get on, not without travelling for hours to and from a distant location. The only option for many of these children is telehealth, which assumes they have access to the required technology and other resources. A late-2022 Senate inquiry further acknowledged that the incidence of school refusal may be highest in areas of great socioeconomic disadvantage, and where parents are also experiencing high rates of anxiety and depression—these parents face the same challenges in seeking help.

Helping these families begins with accessible information and raising awareness of the problem. This includes distinguishing between defiance behaviours or naughtiness and mental health issues, and helping parents to understand why their child is refusing to go to school. Identifying cases early will enable families to intervene before children fall so far behind that it feels almost impossible to catch up. Schools can also work in partnership with parents to help children who are struggling. To address these issues, governments are now listening to the voices of those on the front line, including children with lived experience of the issue, parents, mental health practitioners, and educators.

The Toll on Social Skills

Several years of social distancing and other restrictions, while imposed to ensure health and safety, took a huge toll on our children's development of social and emotional skills. If in 2019 you had asked a child what 'social distancing' meant, you would have been met with a blank stare. If you ask the same question today, a child will readily explain the rules that governed their life in the pandemic. They are still struggling to unlearn these behaviours and interact with others.

The most impacted are our youngest children, the four- and five-year olds who have only just started school and for whom lockdowns impacted almost half of their lives and all of their memories. For these young children, teachers note a greater reliance on adults for simple tasks, trouble reading and processing emotions, and reduced confidence in group activities and in forming new friendships. Teachers also report more aggressive outbursts, such as biting and hitting, by those who feel overwhelmed around large groups of peers. Some children still struggle to read and understand facial expressions, making it difficult for them to pick up social cues from those around them. The contact sport—or contact play for younger children—that helps kids maintain and build friendships with others, remains absent from many social gatherings, as children still fear being too close to others, because of the potential health risk. The implications include increased aggression, sleep problems and feelings of loneliness. This lack of socially acceptable physical interactions means that children aren't learning *not to* hit, *not to* bite, or how and why their actions might hurt someone else.

The development of social skills begins in the first weeks of life and grows exponentially in the early childhood years. These skills include the ability to understand your own emotions—excitement, happiness, fear or embarrassment—and to empathise with other people's perspectives, which encompasses being aware of how to be accountable for mistakes, apologise when in the wrong, and develop social relationships through play. Children typically learn these skills through interactions with others and by engaging in new activities that add to their palette of experiences of the world around them. Without a doubt, the pandemic took this away from many children, whose worlds then became very narrow and boring. Stay-at-home rules kept children safe, but they also robbed them of the breadth of life experiences needed for healthy social growth.

The developmental lag we are now seeing is manifesting in many different ways. For some families, it involves daily tantrums when trying to get their child off to school or away from screens. These externalised behaviours have increased in children between seven and nine years of age, markedly in boys. By contrast, girls are more likely to demonstrate internalising behaviours such as anxiety, fearfulness, depression and social withdrawal. Regardless, in both scenarios, children physically withdraw from interactions with others. It is hoped these behaviours are transient and will be replaced in time by new habits and social networks as children grow in confidence. However, for those children who were already struggling with poor social skills and difficult family circumstances prior to COVID, there is a bigger mountain to climb.

Consider the unique experience of young children with developmental delays such as autism, who entered school with reduced social skills. For some of these children, social isolation during lockdown may have been a positive experience compared to their non-autistic peers. In particular, they didn't have to navigate daily interactions with different people, and life may have moved at a much more manageable pace. For others, where routine was the key, the changes in established daily practices created intense disruption at home and eliminated opportunities for social integration. Some may not even have seen another person outside of their immediate family for lengthy periods—for these kids, already struggling with new people and environments, adjusting to a return to school would have been nothing less than traumatic.

For all children, the summer of 2022 was a significant milestone as they returned to a physical school environment, and began the long journey to adapt to new rules and build new relationships. How can we help them make up for lost time and build critical social skills, whatever circumstances they might be in? The good news is that children are, on the whole, resilient and adaptable. In the short term, three critical areas will need to be focused on in the race to get children socialised again: developing the confidence to establish social relationships and independence; switching from a dependency on online communication; and increasing physical activity and teamwork.

Strained Friendships

The return to classrooms saw educators witness a different dynamic between children. They were particularly concerned by the lack of assurance in children when interacting with others. For younger children in particular, this manifested in difficulties cooperating with instructions, sharing with peers, communicating and listening. The collateral damage of the stress and uncertainty of lockdowns was, and continues to be, children's confidence. This has been evident in the classroom, playground and at home, with children having trouble getting along with others, wanting to be alone, and becoming irritable and angry when they are forced to interact. Remember that, for a six-year-old child, the pandemic spanned more than one-third of their life. After spending such a huge portion of their life coping with restrictions, any readjustment is going to be difficult.

Two of the greatest challenges for children of all ages post-pandemic have been forging new friendships and maintaining old friendships, especially when the ways in which these friends interact and play together has changed so drastically over and over again. Friendships formed in person may not have survived the transition to online learning, and vice versa.

'Katie' was in late primary school when the pandemic hit. She and her best friend had been inseparable since early primary school, always spending time together both in and out of school. But with the pandemic physically isolating them from one another, they were only able to communicate through text messages. The girls struggled to maintain their rapport online and they began to grow apart, often having minor arguments over texts as they each misinterpreted what the other was saying. Their relationship only got worse as restrictions eased, and when they did return to school, their friendship had not recovered. There was now an awkwardness and tension; they did not know how to act around each other or how to rekindle what they'd once had.

Like Katie, many children have returned to school and found that friendships have changed. Two years of not playing games together, not going to birthday parties, not being around each other even when doing nothing, have meant that children have had to relearn how to initiate interactions and begin the difficult process of making friends. Certainly for families who did not have access to digital technologies during the pandemic, friendships that had been formed in person would have been difficult to continue. The move to online learning interactions meant there were no more comfortable silences, nor time spent together without an agenda.

Without friendship comes loneliness. Children thrive in community environments, with meaningful connections being vital to their health and wellbeing. Loneliness increases the risk of mental health problems such as excessive worry, trouble sleeping and intense sadness. It can also have a negative effect on a child's academic achievement, their self-esteem, and communication with friends and family. Loneliness, like other social issues, has been seen to permeate the post-pandemic world, with the potential to become a cycle of detachment and social anxiety that, if unbroken, can have a long-term impact on mental health.

How can we, no matter our role in the community, help children to become confident again, to develop friendships and reduce loneliness? Parents play a critical role in helping their children become social beings. They are the facilitators of opportunities to meet other children, and they become the source of all knowledge on what to expect from, and how to navigate, social interactions. Building friendships is not always a straightforward or easy process, and children also need to relearn how to navigate the rejection and embarrassment of failed attempts at connection. Their ability to cope with this and to build their social resilience comes in part from observing how parents and other family members and adults interact with their own friends. Likewise the return to school which, while it has been difficult for many, has also provided a much-needed opportunity to restart or bolster social relationships.

Screen Dependency

One of the most frequently reported lifestyle changes for children during the pandemic was the excessive time spent on screens and digital media. This included time spent on TVs, e-games, digital tablets and smartphones. In 2019, the 'Australian 24-hour movement guidelines' published by the Department of Health and Aged Care recommended that children aged between five and seventeen engage in less than two hours of sedentary recreational screen time per day. Why is this recommendation so important?

Even prior to the pandemic, concerning links had been found between excessive screen time and poor physical and mental health. In terms of physical well-being, obesity is one of the most well-documented health concerns associated with excessive screen use by children. For children today, screen time is replacing time spent in the real world exploring nature, trying sports, having fun in playgrounds, and simply being around others.

Increased screen time is also associated with poor sleep. Every human being needs sleep, with research documenting that children ideally need 9–11 hours per night—more than their parents, who typically only require 7–9 hours per night. A new issue has arisen recently surrounding the light exposure associated with digital devices. Blue light, the common backlight of smartphones and laptops, is of particular concern as it suppresses melatonin, a hormone necessary for uninterrupted sleep. This is in addition to the endless scrolling through social media and online content that causes sleep delays and can hinder a full night's sleep, making a child restless and tired the next day.

It is not just the device itself that is problematic, but also the content children are viewing on their devices. The rise in social media has given us a new ability to communicate with others anywhere in the world, but it has also given us the ability to compare ourselves to everyone else. Where adults may have some ability to navigate the online world without much self-comparison, children are less equipped to differentiate between what is a real expectation and what are fake or unachievable standards. This has led to a sharp increase in body image issues, especially from self-comparison with heavily photoshopped or staged images of so-called 'real people'. For girls in particular, viewing unrealistic images of female beauty standards can lead to lower self-esteem and progress to body dysmorphia and eating disorders. For boys, meanwhile, extended screen time is correlated with increased frustration and aggression, leading to the acting out of behaviours both at home and at school.

For all children, excessive screen time can have a longlasting impact on attention and focus, mainly because the most popular media content being consumed by children is short videos, sometimes only a few seconds long. This becomes concerningly evident as children enter school for the first time. The capacity to attend to classroom instructions and to focus on details are fundamental building blocks in the development of early literacy and numeracy skills, but this cannot be achieved in a few seconds or in the same engaging manner as a video clip. Children who are unable to sustain attention over a longer period will continue through primary school at a disadvantage to their more attentive peers, facing further problems when they confront more complex material in later education. We are seeing evidence of this now as children progress into high school, and there is reason to believe that, without intervention, these issues may continue throughout their lives.

You might assume that an easy solution is to just reduce or eliminate screen time. However, as we saw throughout the COVID-19 pandemic, a reliance on digital tools is in many ways unavoidable. According to a 2022 study, the average amount of time children spent using screens rose by an alarming 52 per cent from 1 January 2020 to 5 March 2022, equivalent to an extra eighty-four minutes per day.[13] With the permitted time spent on screens having increased during lockdowns to allow for online-only education, it is now a big ask to expect children to reduce their reliance on screens without structured intervention and reasoning. Attempts to do this unassisted lead to behavioural outbursts and tantrums, sapping parents' energy and eroding their ability to enforce rules and restrictions. We are seeing almost a detox-type behaviour from children forced to be without their devices, which is not surprising considering how ingrained screen use has become. In some ways, it is now an addictive reliance, having transitioned in the pandemic from an add-on to daily life, to being at the core of daily life.

It is important for parents and educators alike, as they struggle to keep children off their devices, to remember that things like phones, social media and online games are deliberately designed to be addictive sources of dopamine and distraction. The biggest resource for any tech company or service is time spent by consumers using their tool—and for our children, this means most of their time. Targeted education and media campaigns are needed to raise awareness of this, along with first-step activities such as asking children to note how much time they spend each day sleeping, eating and being absorbed in a screen.

The message for all struggling parents out there is that you are competing against multibillion-dollar companies for your child's attention. Just remember it is a habit, and like all habits, it will take time and patience to break.

A Lack of Activity

The sharp increase in screen time has coincided with an equally sharp decrease in children's physical activity levels, in organised sports and unrestricted play. When children participate in any physical activity, they reduce their risk of developing obesity and poor heart health later in life. But in 2022, only 10 per cent of Australian children were meeting the guideline of one hour of physical activity per day, compared with 19 per cent in 2018. Prior to the pandemic, the Australian Sport and Physical Activity Participation survey, or AUSPLAY, found that 72.7 per cent of children aged five to eleven participated in some form of physical activity outside of school each week. This figure dropped to 63.3 per cent in 2022, as both children and community clubs struggled to return to pre-pandemic norms.

To help children move more and access facilities, state governments have offered reduced registration fees and vouchers for children to participate in organised sport, acknowledging that a cost-of-living crisis is taking its toll on families across Australia. In 2023, the Victorian Government, through its Get Active Kids Voucher Program, made participation in organised sports much more accessible, with $200 vouchers being supplied to families for use at over 1600 activity providers across the state. Further initiatives to promote physical education at 300 disadvantaged government schools in Victoria via $3000 vouchers (one voucher per school) are underway. Similarly, first implemented in 2011, the Western Australian Government's KidSport initiative helps families register their children at sporting clubs with $150 vouchers.

To date, more than 100 000 children aged between five and eighteen have benefited from this initiative.

While these initiatives are helping, however, it seems progress is slow, which begs the question: with some government support available to encourage families to be more involved in sporting or physical activity programs outside of school, what is holding them back? The answer is time—and if not time, then money. The cost of participation, both in time and dollars, will always be a critical decision-making factor, especially for families with multiple children or who are already struggling to make ends meet. These families are further impacted by the rising cost of living, and the seemingly endless recent rises in interest rates in the looming shadow of a recession. The vouchers help, but not enough. With many families working more hours to cover mounting expenses, asking them to then take their children to and from extracurricular activities is unrealistic.

In addition to this, the biggest advocates for this activity, the children themselves, are not as enthusiastic or as motivated to be part of a group activity now, particularly when they could spend that time online. For many children, two years inside a very confined, limited world has diminished a love of such activities and the interactions they involve. When children do return to sports or clubs, we see changes in behaviour such as a reluctance to follow simple etiquette for social interaction and to show basic respect for each other. Higher levels of anxiety have also seen more young children struggle to leave their parents behind when they attend even a one-hour class. Others are more distracted, often not listening to or remembering short instructions, which can cause embarrassment and lead them to resent participating in activities.

A Social Anxiety Pandemic

Without a doubt, the pandemic affected every child in some way. For some, it had its positives, such as more time to spend with families and ongoing communication with friends through the virtual world. But for many thousands of children in Australia, across all states and territories, pandemic-related stress and anxiety rose in the wake of the sudden disruption to their core social and emotional scaffold—school. This disruption has left a mark on the developing brain. Gone in an instant were the casual hallway conversations with friends, school excursions and camps, and team sports. In their place, two years of remote learning and social isolation.

By the time schools reopened in 2022, social anxiety in young children had soared, and many had to regain basic social skills. Those who entered the education system for the first time in the summer of

2020 never had a chance to learn the basic routines of school life, and now, at the age of eight, these children are struggling to adapt. It is sometimes easy to forget that this 'temporary disruption' represented a quarter of their lives.

A 2022 survey of over 5000 families and 130 schools, conducted by Camp Australia, revealed almost a quarter of parents were concerned that their child's emotional wellbeing had continued to decline in 2022, even though the lockdowns had ended. At this time, teachers also reported that when children returned to school, 60 per cent of them were more sensitive and easily overwhelmed.

'Jay', a student who endured Melbourne's lockdowns during his formative years of primary school, suffered from anxiety prior to the pandemic. The return to school post-lockdowns was accompanied by an increase in this anxiety. Jay almost had to be dragged into school. He didn't want to be in a classroom with other children and was worried that his mother wouldn't be waiting for him after school.

In the clinical and research realm of psychology, these behaviours and reactions are classed as social anxiety, which includes the fear of social situations, such as going to school or meeting new people, and is often accompanied by a loss of appetite, nausea and poor sleep. For some children, this fear dissipated within weeks of their re-entering school, but others are still avoiding friends, classmates and teachers almost entirely.

In 2023, there has been a renewed focus on how children are adapting to being back at school. Now a year out of lockdown and starting to settle into a new routine, many children have started to improve and will, hopefully, soon return to what is considered a normal and functional level of behaviour, growing out of the feelings embedded during the pandemic. However, a small subset of children are desperately struggling and need targeted support to try and make the small gains their peers are achieving on their own. These are children who were likely suffering from social anxiety prior to the pandemic and are experiencing additional trauma such as the death of a loved one, family violence or poverty. In some ways, the pandemic hid these problems from teachers and broader support networks, and it is only now, as we return to the 'new normal', that we again start to recognise the children who are being left behind. So what can be done, right now, to help these kids?

How many of us know how to appropriately and confidently talk about our own emotions? Many people go through their entire adult lives never truly addressing their own mental health concerns. As such, we need to remember that young children do not know how to talk about their feelings. They do not know how to explain why they feel down, why they don't want to play with friends or siblings, why they don't want to go to school. We need to help children articulate how they feel in a manner that is age-appropriate but still effective. We also need to equip parents and teachers to recognise certain behaviours that young children display when they feel sad or afraid, such as having trouble falling asleep and crying more easily, or physical complaints such as stomach pains that worsen when a child is separated from their parents. These behaviours are often dismissed as simply 'acting out', perhaps because it's Monday morning and the child is struggling to get ready for school. However, they can point to serious issues that go beyond a typical reaction to the start of the school week after a weekend playing with friends.

Part of the solution is teaching children what emotions are and what they mean. A child's own awareness of how they are feeling will help them communicate when they are struggling. However, we cannot just rely on children to pick up on these concerns. Parents also have to learn to ask questions and articulate their own feelings. After all, children inevitably learn through what they see and hear at home.

The Fate of the Vulnerable

It's worth refocusing now on the most vulnerable children, those experiencing socioeconomic challenges, health issues, parental unemployment, and inadequate access to space and resources. How are they faring in our post-pandemic world?

The digital divide in Australia became even more apparent during the COVID-19 years with the accelerating digitalisation of the Australian economy. This especially impacted families from low-income households, refugees and migrants, children in rural and remote areas, children experiencing learning difficulties and delays, and Indigenous communities. Of course, the return to classrooms did reduce the reliance on computers and the internet for essential daily learning, and digitally disadvantaged children regained access to resources in the classroom that levelled the playing field amongst students. They no longer needed digital tools to communicate and build relationships, and were once again given a chance, in the classroom, to make friends. However, in the home environment, children without internet access or an appropriate device are still being left behind, unable to complete some homework activities or connect with their friends online outside of school hours.

This persistent digital divide is particularly prominent in regards to children experiencing poverty, with high levels of crossover with other at-risk communities. During the pandemic, temporary relief was provided which eased some of the pressures felt by families struggling to make ends meet. However, as we leave the pandemic behind, we also leave behind various government grants and additional assistance, sending some families back to square one. In addition to this, welcoming us as we emerged from lockdown was a cost-of-living crisis. This has hit families and low-income earners particularly hard, a perfect storm of rising mortgage rates, increased costs of goods, difficulty in finding affordable housing, and a constant push to return to pre-pandemic consumer spending. In 2021, it was estimated by the Futurity Investment Group that thirteen years of public schooling (from ages five to eighteen) would cost parents $74 213, including textbooks, uniforms, laptops, stationery and excursions. By 2023, this had increased to an estimated $84 544. For some families, the cost of sending a child to school is simply unaffordable— especially after factoring in the cost of not having older children around to act as caregivers to younger siblings or other family members.

For Aboriginal and Torres Strait Islander children who were not able to connect as easily with their community, land, or the culture of their ancestors during the lockdowns, the post-pandemic world has meant an opportunity to return to Country and gather with family and communities. In the wake of the pandemic, the National Framework for Protecting Australia's Children released its first action plan for 2023–26. The plan addresses the social determinants of child safety and wellbeing, with a primary focus on families experiencing disadvantage and vulnerability. This includes implementing community-led, redesigned service models for Indigenous families, particularly those with multiple and complex needs, with the goals of ensuring all young people and their families have easy access to the culturally appropriate support they need, and that the services they access are trauma-informed, child-centred and family-focused.

For children from culturally diverse families, particularly those from non-English-speaking families, the return to school has provided welcome exposure to English-speaking environments. This is important, and not just for the completion of final-year studies throughout Australia. English-speaking proficiency for young children of refugee and migrant families is often crucial to communicate with service providers and understand government information only provided in English. Children as young as five can be asked to book appointments, translate letters, and act as medical interpreters for family members who themselves cannot speak or understand English.

For children in disruptive families, the return to school presents them with a safe environment in which to learn. These children can now meet with teachers and adult support networks outside of the home, giving them secure places in which to ask for help. This also provides an opportunity for teachers to see children first-hand, and potentially notice and speak up when something seems wrong.

Children who also lived through natural disasters such as the Black Summer bushfires or experienced intense flooding either prior to or during the pandemic, remain vulnerable. Children are resilient but not invulnerable. Given the cumulative effects of multiple upsets, this population needs to receive specialist support by psychologists trained in childhood trauma. Many children remain in their affected communities, living in temporary accommodation or attending school in pop-up classrooms. Their 'return to normal' is not a reality yet, and will not be for quite some time. It is difficult for children in these communities, along with their families, to forget these catastrophic events, as many face the threat of fire or floods every year.

What this snapshot tells us is that, yes, we have now regained all the little freedoms that brought us happiness on a day-to-day basis prior to the pandemic, such as being out in the community, or just being with friends and family. And it is important to cherish these. We have clawed our way back to a life that resembles what we had in 2019. But this new normal is not without significant issues. Now that the COVID-19 pandemic has passed, we are left with what experts have called an unparalleled mental health crisis in Australian children.

POST-PANDEMIC PRIORITIES

In May 2023, the director-general of WHO, Tedros Adhanom Ghebreyesus, issued the following statement: 'It's therefore with great hope that I declare COVID-19 over as a global health emergency.' This declaration provided huge relief to many millions of people all over the world. But nonetheless there are those who were impacted throughout the pandemic and remain impacted today, and we must consider what their future looks like.

As we look at the world beyond the pandemic, leaving behind fear and uncertainty will be one of the hardest challenges to conquer. Children of all ages, no matter where they live, are being affected by this. In 2023, we see the breadth of their battle wounds. Although normal schooling has resumed, it is the hurdles between home and the school gate that may be the hardest to overcome. These hurdles, built on fear and worry, didn't just disappear when lockdowns ended. Children continue to face them, struggling to even get out of bed, to get dressed, to get ready to go to school. Just the thought of school causes debilitating stress and anxiety for some, particularly those who already were at risk of mental health concerns prior to the pandemic. It is a very concerning reality that some of these children may never return to school.

Lying at the core of the pandemic legacy is a pervasive rise in mental health problems, from mildly traumatised to severely affected. A survey of 1000 psychologists, published by the Australian Psychological Society in November 2022, reported an accelerated increase in mental illness in children aged six to twelve. The sharpest rise occurred in relation to diagnoses of social anxiety disorders (a 45 per cent increase over two years) and ADHD (42 per cent). A prominent repercussion of this is the increased national trend of school refusal. To address this, a Senate inquiry into this issue is currently seeking expert and community opinions on ways to reduce the psychological impact on families, as well as the growing caseload and demands on schools and healthcare providers to support these children.

The current access to and availability of mental health support cannot keep up with this unprecedented crisis among our children. Prior to the pandemic, access to specialist child health care had already been limited in Australia; today, it's at breaking point. If left unchecked, this will force greater isolation on those who cannot readily access affordable, appropriate and inclusive health care. The process of understanding how we can help relieve some of this pressure is underway, but we already know one thing: there is no easy answer. The solution we need will be as complex as the issues we face.

At first glance, a corrective seems obvious: increase the professional workforce by training more psychologists, and build a nationwide digital platform that will provide easy access to services wherever a child lives. But therein lie the problems, four in particular.

Problem number one: immediate psychological help is needed for so many children across Australia. Unfortunately, the process of training and deploying psychologists is not immediate, far from it. Much like the training required to be a physician, it takes years of supervised instruction to become a qualified psychologist. Increasing training positions will only meet the long-term need—we will likely be waiting years before we start to see the fruits of this labour. That said, this increase in mental health professionals remains critical, and we can look at it as better late than never. To kickstart this, the federal government, in its May 2023 Budget, pledged to invest over $91 million in mental health workforce reform over the next five years. This funding includes $56 million for universities to create 500 additional postgraduate psychology places, $27.7 million for 500 one-year internships for provisional psychologists, and $5.9 million for 2000 fully subsidised supervisor training sessions. It sounds like a lot, but is it really enough? Unfortunately, probably not. Given the number of psychology training programs across Australia (well over fifty), spreading this additional funding across all of them will significantly dilute its impact. The truth is that money alone won't fix the immediate problem. Still, it is a significant step in the right direction.

Problem number two: trained psychologists and soon-to-be psychologists are leaving the public health system and moving into private practice. This means that only those with the finances needed to access private health care are getting help quickly, leaving those in the public healthcare system on endless waitlists—some wait up to six months before an appointment is available. This further entrenches the mental health difficulties faced by vulnerable children.

Problem number three: even if we had enough psychologists to see and help every child in need, it is an undeniable fact that most of these psychologists would be located in suburban and inner-city areas, while many of the children in need are not. We cannot expect families to regularly travel hours from home so their children can speak with a mental health professional for an hour. That would mean missed work, additional money and time devoted to travel, and making arrangements for siblings to be cared for. This is a burden for families, and it is a burden for the child who is watching their parents or caregivers struggle, inevitably thinking they are to blame.

Problem number four: while telehealth options such as phone or video psychologist sessions could be utilised to address the travel issue, this is not so straightforward because the issues surrounding access to technology did not disappear when children returned to school. Many families still do not have reliable access to the internet and the relevant technologies, which particularly applies to families in remote areas. And even if they did, access to a psychologist is not the only factor here. Children also need access to a safe, private space where they can take these calls. Some families might be able to make it work; however, for those children whose biggest challenges stem from family relationships, such a space may not be available, especially not at home.

Given all these problems and the urgent need to focus on the present, how exactly can our children get the help they need, right now?

More Mental Health Workers

At the beginning of 2022, we started to see in the news more stories about Australia's dwindling supply of clinical psychologists. Not only did we not have enough, but the ones we did have were experiencing severe burnout and in some cases were closing their client books and leaving the profession. Alongside this was the decision to wind back the additional Medicare-subsidised psychology sessions that had been introduced during the pandemic. Debate has raged since then about the federal government's decision to scale back this support, as it was obvious that the need had not gone away—including the needs of affected children—just because the lockdowns had ended. The government's refusal to revisit this decision has been met with utter disbelief by many mental health experts who warn that even more children will now struggle with post-pandemic life. But while this is a bitter pill to swallow, we can't just sit around discussing decisions that have already been made. For one thing, we shouldn't forget that just because these Medicare subsidies were available, this did not guarantee a family or child would even be able to make a booking or find a qualified and Medicare-supported mental health provider. But more importantly, there remains an urgent need to rethink how we deliver health care so that it quickly gets to children and families in need. This must happen in an affordable, appropriate manner, which includes dealing with the monetary cost, and finding novel ways to expand the capacity of our mental health workforce.

One solution is to truly bring together the multi-disciplinary community of mental health providers in Australia by including the counselling profession in the Medicare Better Access rebate scheme. Its current exclusion from the scheme denies access to afforda-ble mental health support by thousands of families who live in rural and remote regions where higher numbers of counsellors and psychotherapists are based. This ignores the fact that Medicare is one of the only ways many families can access any kind of health support—these same families do not care what type of degree a mental health professional has, only whether or not they can help their child. The reason why counsellors are not currently included in the scheme is because they are not regulated by the Australian Health Practitioner Regulation Agency (AHPRA), the same agency that regulates who can call themselves a doctor, a nurse or a psychologist. It does make sense that without some type of oversight, opening up the Better Access rebate initiative to anyone and everyone who wishes to call themselves a mental health professional would be problematic, but this is not what is being suggested here. Rather, let's find a way to upskill counsellors ethically and professionally, and therefore make them part of AHPRA or another regulated body. Many of these professionals have extensive experience and the invaluable skills necessary to work directly and compassionately with others, and some level of upskilling or integration into the world of Medicare and medical regulation would make these skills affordable, thereby providing a much-needed mental health services pipeline. Doing this acknowledges the outstanding work done by counsellors; increases accessibility for families, especially families in need; and goes a long way towards filling the gap between the help that is available and the help that is needed.

A second solution is to utilise the 15 000 psychology graduates who complete Australia's accredited psychology undergraduate program each year. Currently, only 7 per cent of these graduates obtain a place in a clinical training program, a figure unlikely to change soon. The remainder move into a variety of jobs, most of which leverage their unique skills from a sales and business standpoint, rather than with health support or provision in mind. But what if we boldly stepped forward and seized the opportunity to revolutionise our psychology undergraduate training and create thousands of new, high-quality mental health workers? With an additional six-month postgraduate qualification, and working in partnership with community organisations such as Headspace, Head to Health providers, and other community services including in education, disability, aged care and the National Disability Insurance Scheme, our new workforce would meet the needs of the community in early intervention, prevention and promotion of mental health. This would take quite some pressure off our existing psychology workforce.

This initiative would not serve to replace qualified psychologists but rather exist as an alternative for those who likely would not have made it into the intensely competitive clinical program, but who are nonetheless still passionate about supporting the mental health of their community. These professionals would work alongside psychologists, and supplement initiatives such as the Head to Health program at the federal level, which commenced in 2021, and the recommendations of the final report of the Royal Commission into Victoria's Mental Health System, published in February 2021.[14] Australia would not be the first nation to do this, as the United Kingdom has been a pioneer in this space for over thirty years through the creation of the assistant psychologist role. This has been an incredibly successful initiative that allows graduates to train alongside qualified psychologists to prepare them for work in a variety of roles to support people with mental health conditions. Let's follow their lead, but in our own Australian way.

Accessible Mental Health Support

Everyone in a child's community plays a role in shaping who they are, including by influencing their mental health, wellbeing and resilience. Every stage in a child's life, from beginning primary school to the transition to high school, presents challenges to their emotional, social and psychological health. Promoting good mental health in children, right from the start, can help them build strong friendships, communicate well, and adapt to and overcome challenges. Skills learnt in childhood, such as resilience, flexibility and managing emotions, set children up for their transition into teenage years and eventually into adulthood. Children are active in their homes, schools and communities, so helping them access mental health support in each of these environments is imperative if they are to strengthen their wellbeing in the post-pandemic world.

COVID-19 highlighted the critical need for Australian governments to urgently invest in equipping our families, schools and communities to safeguard our children's mental health and build resilience. But what was the response? What does the governmental report card look like in 2023?

Everyone agrees that schools provide a vital hub for the development of young minds in a safe and nurturing environment. Yet coming back to school has not been easy for many children, with anxiety the most prevalent of all mental health concerns. So equipping teachers to identify early, persistent signs of anxiety is an essential step in ensuring the appropriate support can be given as soon as possible, before the issue becomes a pervasive, clinical problem. Recognising the urgent need to equip teachers to respond to students' mental health needs, the Victorian Department of Education invested $217.8 million in 2021 to develop an evidence-based Schools Mental Health

Menu, known as The Menu. A collaboration between community members, teachers and mental health experts, The Menu contains endorsed programs and resources to support schools to improve the mental health of their students. It aids schools in making informed choices on how to spend their funding, including positive mental health promotion such as the Friendly Schools whole-school emotional and social wellbeing and bullying prevention program. It provides tools for early intervention and age-appropriate support, such as the Brief Interventions in Youth Mental Health Toolkit, a program for training school mental health workers to deliver psychosocial interventions to children. It empowers teachers to take an active role in mental health and wellbeing support in their classroom, and to quickly identify children who need additional assistance. The Menu is also personalised, with culturally appropriate and inclusive programs for Aboriginal and Torres Strait Islander children, as well as for vulnerable children who have lived through traumatic events, and refugee and migrant children. The Menu is now being used in schools across Victoria.

There has been some additional work in Victoria, and Australia-wide, to train and place in schools wellbeing and mental health workers. Alongside The Menu, the Victorian Government is aiming to provide, for each public and low-fee non-public primary school, a trained 'mental health and well-being leader' by 2026. This effort is currently being piloted in approximately a hundred schools, with a rollout anticipated later in 2023, prioritising rural and regional primary schools. At the federal level, additional funds have been provided to support schemes in disadvantaged communities. For example, in 2021, $2.5 million was allocated to train teachers in 600 rural and regional primary schools to become 'mindfulness champions' through the Smiling Mind Schools Program. These small initiatives are designed to create a holistic and safe mental health environment where students feel empowered to seek help.

The COVID-19 pandemic also highlighted the immense amount of mental health support parents and carers provide to children, acting as the default front line of children's support networks. This means parents need to have the appropriate resources at their fingertips if they are to be the support their child needs. Most people do not have any professional or meaningful training in mental health awareness or assistance, and this is not something that is innately learned when you become a parent. We should also recognise that many parents are experiencing degrees of mental health issues themselves, alongside balancing work and keeping a home functioning, and so sometimes parents just do not have the emotional or physical capacity to ensure their child's wellbeing.

One of the most innovative ways to help parents obtain the needed resources is through digital technology and programs created by, for and with researchers and parents. Two gold-standard programs that were given accelerated funding during the pandemic are the Triple P—Positive Parenting Program (https://www. triplep.net) and the Parenting Strategies website (https://www.parentingstrategies.net).

Triple P is an online program that offers parents and caregivers of children aged less than twelve free resources and strategies to build their child's resilience, emotional wellbeing and coping skills. Triple P focuses on helping parents build their own mental health and wellbeing so that they can support their children when needed. Between the program's launch in October 2022 and May 2023, over 100 000 families across the country accessed this parenting resource. It helped them to start the mental health conversation in their households, a vital step towards safeguarding the psychological wellbeing of their children.

The Parenting Strategies website, built by researchers at Monash University and the University of Melbourne, focuses on translating evidence-based research into practical resources and guidelines that are understandable to and applicable by parents. Supported by the National Health and Medical Research Council and Beyond Blue, the website is targeted at helping parents protect their child's mental health, with a focus on supporting the caregiver. Parents are able to access practical guidelines on how to navigate school refusal, and how to help children who are already experiencing mental health challenges such as feelings of anxiety or chronic worry, sadness or hopelessness.

In addition, parents who are struggling to support their children's mental health and wellbeing can contact Parent Line in their state or territory (https://www.parentline.org.au/parent-line-in-other-states). This service is for parents and carers of children up to eighteen years of age. It is also critical that children are able to access support when needed, and that they have the capacity to seek help themselves. Kids Helpline (https://kidshelpline.com.au) provides children with free, private and confidential 24/7 counselling support through a telephone or web chat service, with the ability to contact the same counsellor on multiple occasions, and with no time limit on a session.

The pandemic caused the closure of some community services that children and families relied on, but fortunately some have reopened, including youth centres and programs in most local government areas around the country. These services give kids access to resources and experiences among their peers and neighbours, as well as helping build social support networks that are crucial for children's wellbeing and development. However, to aid those children who are already struggling with mild to moderate mental health issues, and who could benefit from a mental health–specific service, the federal government has committed $54.2 million of funding to the creation of Head to Health Kids Hubs. These aim to support children aged up to twelve, and their families, by improving early intervention outcomes and enhancing service provision. The hubs are designed to be a secondary-level service for emerging and complex issues, and provide culturally appropriate services for Aboriginal and Torres Strait Islander children, as well as children from different cultural backgrounds. The Head to Health Kids Hubs are currently in development, the goal being to establish seventeen hubs across the country by mid-2026. In Victoria, they are known as Infant, Child and Family Health and Wellbeing Hubs, and three of them are expected to open to the public towards the end of 2023.

Improved Digital Access

The switch to telehealth appointments during the pandemic was a game-changer for many families who could not access in-person services. Between March 2020 and July 2022, 95 000 health practitioners delivered more than 118.2 million telehealth services to eighteen million patients. When safe and clinically appropriate, telehealth can be a cost-effective, convenient and accessible alternative to face-to-face health services. The Better Access Telehealth initiative has been in place since late 2017, allowing those in rural and remote communities to utilise these services. For those in urban areas, Medicare-covered telehealth services only became an option in 2020. Initially causing concern that they would paralyse the Medicare system, they are now a permanent and crucial part of the health offerings in Australia.

Although telehealth sessions are still offered over the phone for those without an internet connection, getting access to and organising them is now primarily done online. But what about those who do not have stable and reliable internet access? Or those who have never learned how to use the internet? And what about those who, even if they could organise a phone or video call with a doctor, have nowhere safe or private to take the call? Support packages coordinated by multiple organisations, including state governments, retail service providers and telecommunication companies, are enabling some disadvantaged children to have access to the internet and laptops for school. This allows them and their families to attend telehealth appointments and receive mental health support. But for those who are ineligible for these programs, the digital divide continues to expand, leaving them without the same access to vital health services as others.

There are many large barriers between where we stand now and an Australia where every community has access to the internet. Among the sixty-five recommendations of the Royal Commission into Victoria's Mental Health System is one entitled 'Building a contemporary system through digital technology', which includes a call for the Victorian Government to enable mental health and wellbeing services to offer devices, and internet and digital literacy support, to families who cannot otherwise access digital services. The royal commission further recommended that regulatory arrangements be developed, funding provided, and technology integrated into communities by providers, with support from the Victorian Government. This is an ambitious and valiant goal; however, in many ways, this remains an issue of access, literacy, willingness to take up, and individual circumstances for both providers and clients. Achieving this goal will be a monumental task that will likely require years of dedicated funding and focus from everyone involved. We are unlikely to see this recommendation resolved any time soon, but we remain hopeful.

TOMORROW'S CHILD

We now have the opportunity to redesign our world so that our children can thrive and learn, a task made all the more urgent by the need to prevent our children from falling into a cycle of poor mental health, risk behaviours or substance use, lack of education, and reduced professional and personal opportunities. To rebuild our children's mental health, after the duress experienced during the pandemic, we must redefine how mental health services are delivered to our communities, and create a scaffold of affordable and accessible support. Sustained investments at every level are needed, for generations to come, to ensure our children remain resilient as they move into adolescence and then into adulthood as productive and healthy members of their community. This ongoing investment must not be at the whim of successive governments. It needs to be ingrained in the fabric of our society, in our values and priorities. In many ways this has begun, but it cannot stop and it cannot slow down.

In 2028, which will be eight years on from the arrival of COVID-19 in Australia, today's post-pandemic child will be a teenager. They will face two very different possible scenarios.

Scenario One. These post-pandemic children grow up to see themselves as the 'lost generation' whose lives changed forever in the shadow of COVID-19. After an initial steep investment in mental health services, by as early as 2026 this new era of initiatives embracing people and technology has been forgotten, and any initial gains have died out. By 2028, further leaps in technology and digital tools have left disadvantaged and vulnerable children behind. They are even more discriminated against, and the daily pressures on their mental health and wellbeing, without any support, threaten to obliterate them. Every year, a new 'unprecedented' number of children in need is announced, and the gap between what is needed and what is offered continues to grow. Limited investment in training teachers and parents in the early detection and prevention of mental health problems now hits home in the form of rampant anxiety disorders, major depression and ADHD, shattering our public and private health services. With these on their knees, only those with the most resources are able to access the help they need, ensuring that families and their future opportunities continue to be defined by socioeconomic status. Poor mental health and school refusals then cascade into a deleterious pathway of school dropouts, substance abuse and isolation, narrowing vocational opportunities at every step. Not only does this impact our teenagers, but it also impacts, from a government standpoint, our future workers—if communities and individuals cannot flourish, neither can a national economy.

Scenario Two. Our children grow up to see themselves as a generation positively defined by the pandemic. Where they once faced challenges, they have now grown resilient. Investments in mental health prevention in pre-schools and primary schools are maintained, with teachers working in partnership with families to raise awareness of early signs and symptoms of issues. By 2028, this model has been adopted in high schools across Australia, ensuring mental health support and resources are ongoing throughout a child's entire school years. The incidence of youth-related mental health disorders remains stable, and school refusals return to pre-COVID levels, avoiding the predicted deepening of the so-called 'shadow pandemic' of lifetime mental illness. Teenagers, through education and support networks, transition into adulthood without the scars of dangerous and life-threatening risk behaviours and substance use. Although initially requiring onerous government investment in mental health services, these people have now evolved into a school force and future workforce of psychologically well and productive Australians. The awareness of and interest in mental health across the community has inspired commercial investments in digital mental health and other homegrown initiatives, all combining to build the Australian economy and our society.

Australia is on the brink of transformational change. Let's make sure it happens, for the sake of our children.

ACKNOWLEDGEMENTS

I have been a researcher in child development for over thirty years. Throughout those years, at all stages of my career, I have been privileged to work with gifted researchers across three continents. I would like to give my profound thanks to two Monash University early career researchers who will in time make a huge impact on our world in the work they pursue: Isabelle Smart and Melinda McCabe. You helped shape this book. You were both brilliant.

I would also like to acknowledge the tremendous work and dedication of our nation's teachers. They guided our children through an incredible period of uncertainty and upheaval. They adopted in a heartbeat new ways to engage and motivate young learners, some of whom were starting school for the first time, and they had to find novel ways to support those with limited access to technology. They were our backbone.

Finally, I would like to thank my family, John, Luke, Holly, Michael and Nicola, for all your support and pride in what I do.

NOTES

1   Max Hirshkowitz, Kaitlyn Whiton, Steven M Albert, Cathy Alessi, Oliviero Bruni, Lydia DonCarlos, Nancy Hazen et al., 'National Sleep Foundation's Sleep Time Duration Recommendations: Methodology and Results Summary', *Sleep Health*, vol. 1, no. 1, 2015, pp. 40–3, https://doi.org/10.1016/j.sleh.2014.12.010 (viewed July 2023).

2   Tracy Evans-Whipp and Constantine Gasser, *Growing up in Australia: The Longitudinal Study of Australian Children (LSAC) Annual Statistical Report 2018*, Australian Institute of Family Studies, Melbourne, 2018, https://growingupinaustralia.gov.au/research-findings/annual-statistical-reports-2018 (viewed July 2023).

3   Maggie Yu and Jennifer Baxter, *The Study of Australian Children Annual Statistical Report*, Australian Institute of Family Studies, Melbourne, 2016, https://growingupinaustralia.gov.au/research-findings/annual-statistical-report-2015/australian-childrens-screen-time-and-participation-extracurricular (viewed July 2023).

4   Australian Government Department of Health and Aged Care, 'Physical Activity and Exercise Guidelines for All Australians', 2021, https://www.health.gov.au/topics/physical-activity-and-exercise/physical-activity-and-exercise-guidelines-for-all-australians (viewed July 2023).

5   Australian Institute of Health and Welfare, *Australia's Children*, Australian Institute of Health and Welfare, Canberra, 2020.

6   B Williamson, F Markham and JK Weir, *Aboriginal Peoples and the Response to the 2019–2020 Bushfires*, Centre for Aboriginal Economic Policy Research, Australian National University, Canberra, 2020, https://doi.org/10.25911/5e7882623186c (viewed July 2023).

7   Bhiamie Williamson, *Aboriginal Community Governance on the Frontlines and Faultlines in the Black Summer Bushfires*, Centre for Aboriginal Economic Policy Research, Australian National University, Canberra, December 2021, https://doi.org/10.25911/V482-AE70 (viewed July 2023).

8   Timothy Heffernan, Emily Macleod, Lisa-Marie Greenwood, Iain Walker, Jo Lane, Samantha Stanley, Olivia Evans, Alison Calear and Tegan Cruwys, *Mental Health, Wellbeing and Resilience after the 2019-20 Bushfires: The Australian National Bushfire Health and Wellbeing Survey: A Preliminary Report*, Research School of Psychology, Australian National University, December 2022, https://doi.org/10.25911/AG7D-7574 (viewed July 2023).

9   Julian Thomas, Jo Barraket, Sharon Parkinson, Chris Wilson, Indigo Holcombe-James, Jenny Kennedy, Kate Mannell and Abigail Brydon, 'Measuring Australia's Digital Divide: Australian Digital Inclusion Index 2021', RMIT University, Swinburne University of Technology and Telstra, 2021, https://doi.org/10.25916/PHGW-B725 (viewed July 2023).

10 Peter Davidson, Bruce Bradbury and Melissa Wong, *Poverty in Australia 2022: A Snapshot*, Australian Council of Social Service and UNSW Sydney, 2022.

11 The Royal Children's Hospital Melbourne, *COVID-19 Pandemic: Effects on the Lives of Australian Children and Families*, RCH National Child Health Poll, Parkville, Vic., 2020.

12 Australian Government Department of Education, *Australian Early Development Census National Report 2021: Early Childhood Development in Australia*, Commonwealth of Australia, Canberra, 2022.

13 Sheri Madigan, Rachel Eirich, Paolo Pador, Brae Anne McArthur and Ross D Neville, 'Assessment of Changes in Child and Adolescent Screen Time During the COVID-19 Pandemic: A Systematic Review and Meta-Analysis', *JAMA Pediatrics*, vol. 176, no. 12, 1 December 2022, pp. 1188–98, https://doi.org/10.1001/jamapediatrics.2022.4116 (viewed July 2023).

14 State of Victoria, *Royal Commission into Victoria's Mental Health System: Final Report*, Melbourne, 2021, http://www.rcvmhs.vic.gov.au (viewed July 2023).